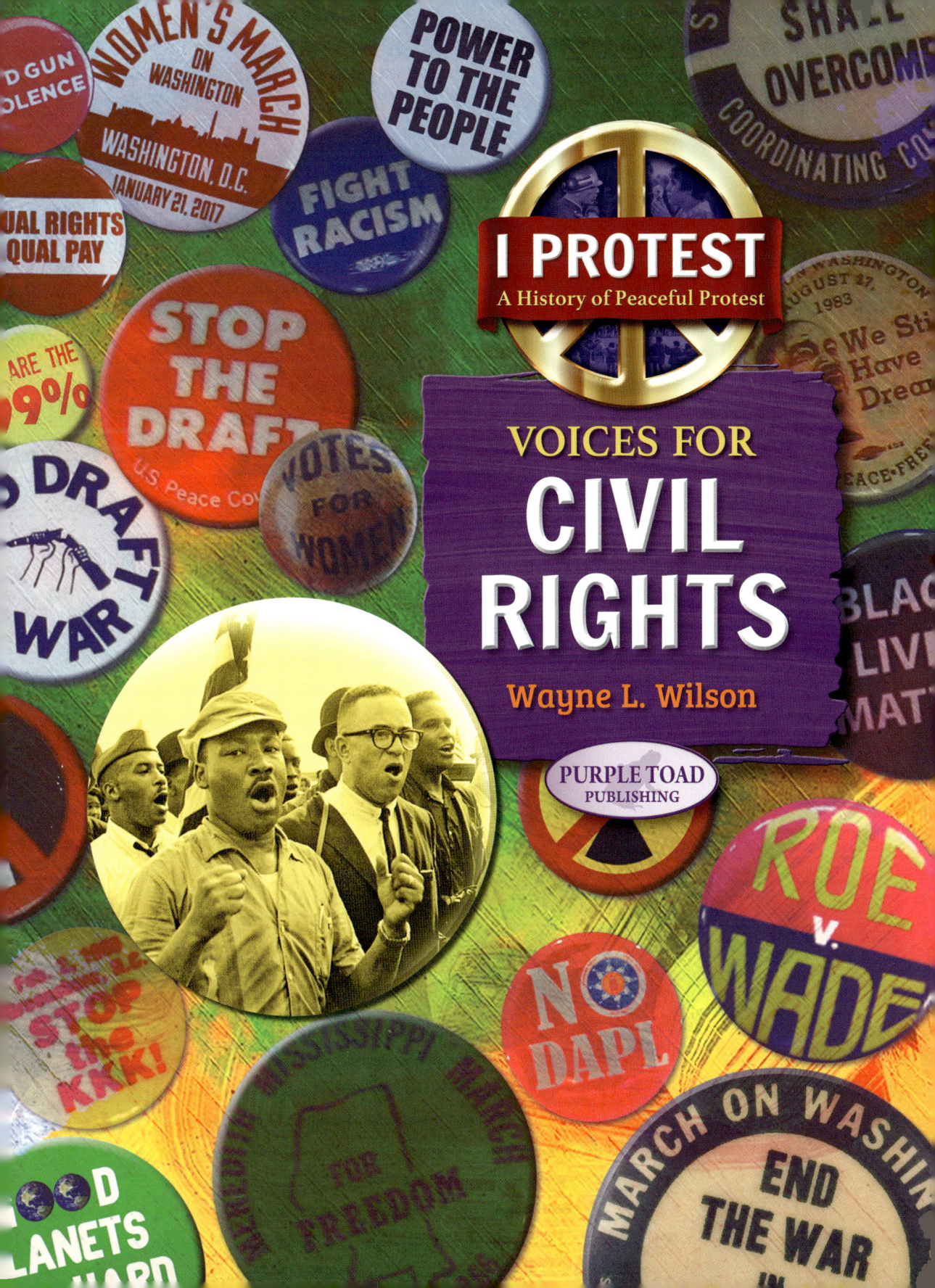

Copyright © 2018 by Purple Toad Publishing, Inc. All rights reserved. No part of this book may be reproduced without written permission from the publisher. Printed and bound in the United States of America.

Printing   1   2   3   4   5   6   7   8   9

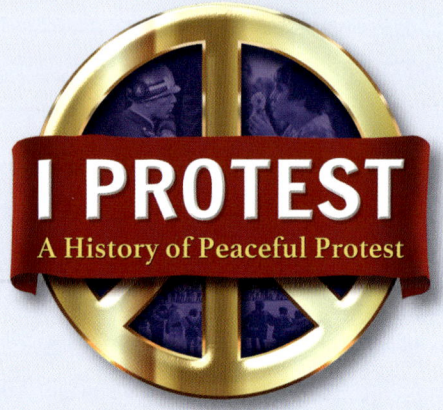

Voices for Civil Rights
by Wayne L. Wilson

Voices for the Environment
by Tamra B. Orr

Voices for Equality
by Tamra B. Orr

Voices for Freedom
by Michael DeMocker

Voices for Peace
by Wayne L. Wilson

ABOUT THE AUTHOR
Wayne L. Wilson has written numerous biographical and historical books for children and young adults. He received a Master of Arts in Education with a specialization in Sociology and Anthropology from UCLA. He is also a screenwriter and member of the Writer's Guild of America.

Publisher's Cataloging-in-Publication Data
Wilson, Wayne L.
  Voices for civil rights / written by Wayne L. Wilson.
     p. cm.
Includes bibliographic references, glossary, and index.
ISBN 9781624693793
1. Passive resistance—History—Juvenile literature. 2. Civil disobedience—Juvenile literature. 3. Social action—Juvenile literature. 4. African Americans—Civil rights—Juvenile literature. 5. Civil rights movements—United States—History—20th century—Juvenile literature. I. Series: I protest.
  E185.615 2017
  323.7

Library of Congress Control Number: 2017940580

ebook ISBN: 9781624693809

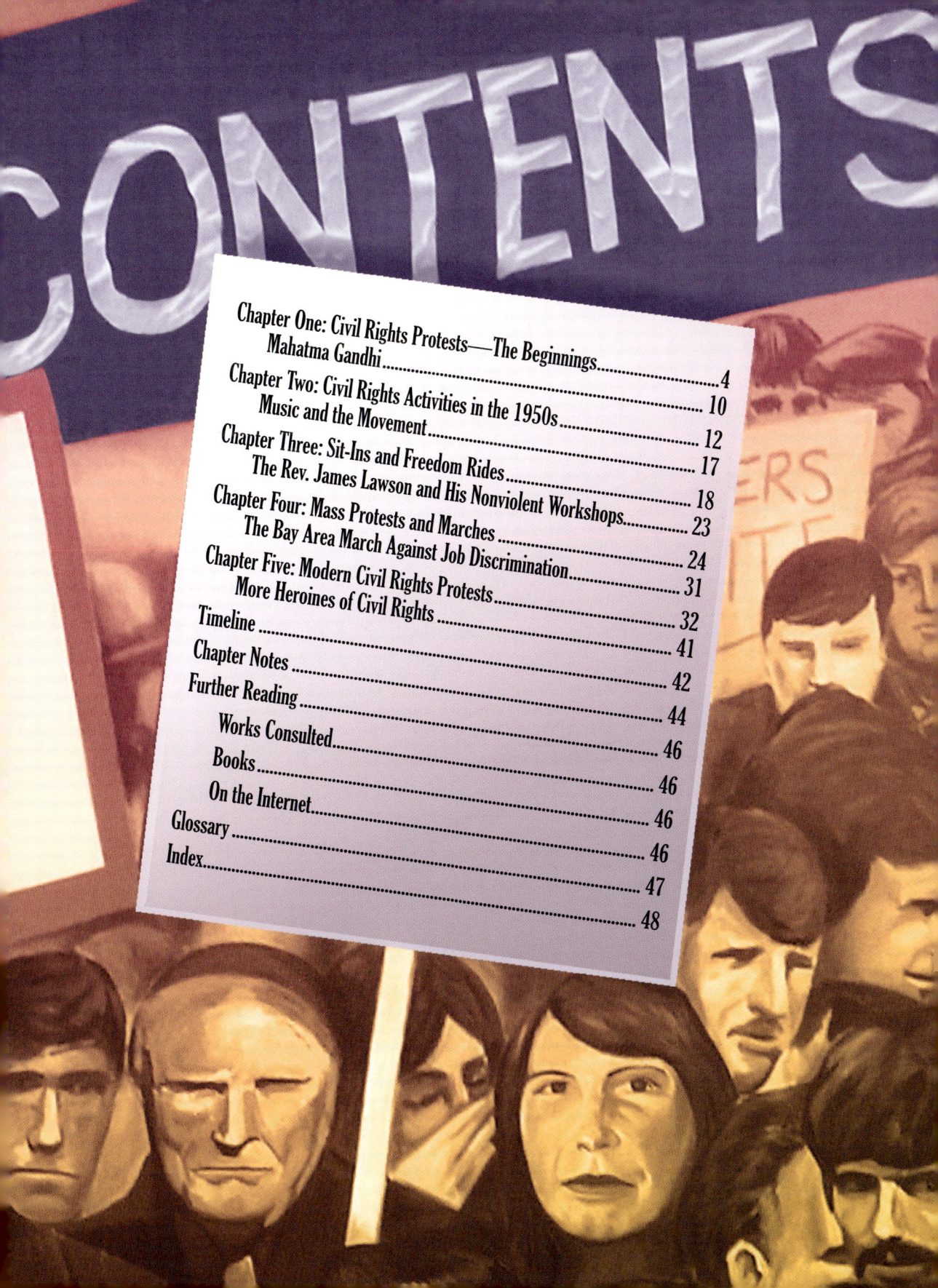

Contents

Chapter One: Civil Rights Protests—The Beginnings 4
   Mahatma Gandhi 10
Chapter Two: Civil Rights Activities in the 1950s 12
   Music and the Movement 17
Chapter Three: Sit-Ins and Freedom Rides 18
   The Rev. James Lawson and His Nonviolent Workshops 23
Chapter Four: Mass Protests and Marches 24
   The Bay Area March Against Job Discrimination 31
Chapter Five: Modern Civil Rights Protests 32
   More Heroines of Civil Rights 41
Timeline 42
Chapter Notes 44
Further Reading 46
   Works Consulted 46
   Books 46
   On the Internet 46
Glossary 47
Index 48

CHAPTER 1
Civil Rights Protests— The Beginnings

If there is no struggle, there is no progress.

—Frederick Douglass[1]

The history of the African American civil rights movement features brave individuals and groups of people. At times the battles against racism and prejudice have led to violence; but many famous victories for equal rights were the result of passive resistance.

In the early nineteenth century in the United States, black and white abolitionists publicly protested against slavery and racial injustice. They wrote and distributed pamphlets and newspapers demanding an end to slavery. Women walked door to door in many northern neighborhoods, asking people to sign their antislavery petitions.

The *Birth of a Nation* Protest

At the start of the twentieth century, a new civil rights organization was formed. It was called the National Association for the Advancement of Colored People (NAACP). The organization's purpose was to fight against racial discrimination

On April 11, 1851, abolitionist Wendell Phillips protested the case of fugitive slave, Thomas Sims, from being returned to slavery. His effort failed. Sims was shipped back to Savannah and publicly whipped.

CHAPTER ONE

and to provide equal rights for all people. Its black and white founders included W.E.B. Du Bois, Mary White Ovington, Ida B. Wells-Barnett, and Dr. Henry Moscowitz.[2]

One of the NAACP's early national campaigns was against D.W. Griffith's groundbreaking film *The Birth of a Nation*. Based on the 1905 book *The Clansmen*, this racist film glorified the Ku Klux Klan. African Americans were shown in the film as rapists, dumb politicians, and stupidly loyal servants. Black characters were played by white people in blackface. President Woodrow Wilson, a segregationist, highly praised the film when it premiered in early 1915. The NAACP wanted the film to be censored.[3]

W.E.B. Du Bois and poster for *The Birth of a Nation*

In 1915, William Monroe Trotter, civil rights leader and editor of *The Guardian* newspaper, opposed the film when it showed in Boston. Trotter and the NAACP staged 18 mass rallies ranging from 500 to 2,500 protesters each. They demonstrated in front of Boston's Faneuil Hall, rallied on the Boston Common, marched on the State House, and held picket signs in front of Boston's Tremont Theater.[4]

Even though the film was considered a success, some cities refused to show it because of the demonstrations. Activists realized there was power in mass protests. Membership in the NAACP tripled.

The East St. Louis Riot Protest

In East St. Louis, Illinois, on July 2, 1917, violence broke out after a failed strike at the Aluminum Ore Company. When white workers went on strike

Civil Rights Protests—The Beginnings

to protest labor conditions, the company hired black workers to replace them. Furious, white mobs burned buildings and attacked black men, women, and children. Up to 200 people were killed and hundreds injured during this bloody riot. Thousands of blacks fled from their homes in fear.

The NAACP conducted its first major civil rights protest. Led by lawyer James Weldon Johnson, 10,000 black men, women, and children marched down Fifth Avenue in New York City in a "Silent Protest Parade."[5]

The New York Times described the Saturday march as "one of the most orderly demonstrations ever witnessed on Fifth Avenue." About 20,000 blacks and some whites lined the route. They watched in silence as people marched 36 blocks from Fifty-ninth Street and Fifth Avenue to Madison Square Park near the Flatiron Building. The only sound was the slow muffled beating of drums.[6]

The NAACP organized a Silent Parade on July 28, 1917, in response to the East St. Louis riots. Ten thousand African Americans participated in this protest march. In the front row are James Weldon Johnson (far right) and W.E.B. Du Bois (second from right).

CHAPTER ONE

Eight hundred children dressed in white led the parade. Next came women, also dressed in white. The men dressed in black. Their banners and signs read: "Mother, do lynchers go to heaven?"; "Give me a chance to live"; "Color, blood, and suffering have made us one"; and "America has lynched without trial 2,867 Negroes in 31 years and not a single murderer has suffered."

The Jack Spratt Diner Sit-In

The first organized civil rights "sit-in" in American history happened in May 1942. A local diner in Chicago, Jack Spratt, would not serve black customers. James Farmer studied Indian nationalist leader Mohandas Gandhi's strategy of nonviolent action. He decided to test this approach on the diner. He, George Houser, and Bernice Fisher formed a group named the Committee of Racial Equality (CORE). They would protest with a sit-in.

Twenty-eight people entered Jack Spratt in groups of two, three, and four. In each party there was at least one black man or woman.[7] In these groups, no whites ate until the black people were served. In some groups, the whites would hand their plate to the black person nearest them. The manager offered to serve all the "colored" people in the basement if they would go there, but the customers politely refused. Next, the manager offered to serve them if they would move to the back corner of the diner. He was again declined. The frustrated manager phoned the police. The

James Farmer in 1965. His actions earned him the Presidential Medal of Freedom in 1998.

Civil Rights Protests—The Beginnings

police refused to kick the group out and left. Finally, the CORE members were served the food they ordered.

CORE went back to the restaurant days later and found that Jack Spratt's policy of not serving African Americans had changed. It was a small but important victory.

The Journey of Reconciliation

In 1946, the Supreme Court declared that segregation in interstate travel was unconstitutional. But this ruling was largely ignored in the South. In 1947, CORE sent eight white and eight black men into the South by bus and train. Activists George Houser and Bayard Rustin organized the two-week "Journey of Reconciliation" through Virginia, North Carolina, Tennessee, and Kentucky.

Bayard Rustin (center, wearing bowtie), George Houser (front, black suit), and other members of the Journey of Reconciliation stand outside the office of Attorney S. W. Robinson. They made the first Freedom Ride in 1947.

Blacks sat in the front and whites in the back. Twelve arrests were made for violating the state's Jim Crow laws.[8] In North Carolina, Bayard Rustin and Andrew Johnson were sentenced to thirty days on a chain gang. The judge was harsher with Joe Felmet and Igal Roodenko, two white Jews from New York. The judge said, "Just to teach you a lesson, I gave your black boys thirty days, and I gave you ninety!"[9]

The Journey of Reconciliation received a lot of media attention. In1948, Houser and Rustin were honored with the Thomas Jefferson Award for the Advancement of Democracy. They received the award because of their efforts to end segregation in interstate travel.

Mahatma Gandhi

Gandhi, spiritual leader of the Indian Independence Movement, said: "You must be the change you wish to see in the world."

Mohandas Karamchand Gandhi was born in India in 1869 to an upper-class Hindu family. Known as Mahatma (Great Soul), Gandhi led India to independence from British rule. His belief in passive resistance for change inspired many great civil rights leaders, including Martin Luther King, Jr. and Nelson Mandela.

Gandhi's activism began as a young lawyer in South Africa. He was shocked and angered about how horribly Indians were treated by the white British government. In his first court appearance in 1893, he was asked to remove his turban. He refused and walked out of the courtroom. Days later a white man complained about Gandhi sitting in the first-class section of a train. Though he had a ticket, he was thrown off the train at the next station. It was then he vowed to fight the "deep disease of color prejudice."[10]

Gandhi studied world religions and Hindu spiritual books. He said, "The religious spirit within me became a living force."[11] He chose to live a simple life. He spun his own clothes with a spinning wheel. He ate vegetarian food and devoted time to prayer, fasting, and meditation.

One of the religious principles he learned was *ahimsa* (a-him-sa), meaning, "doing no harm." Gandhi turned it into a nonviolent tool to resist oppression. Gandhi called it *satyagraha* (sat-YAH-graha)—"truth force." Gandhi believed the purpose of using nonviolence as a weapon was to change that person's point of view, to win over his or her mind and heart.[12]

In South Africa and India, Gandhi organized nonviolent protests against the British Empire. His campaigns involved peaceful demonstrations, sit-ins, picketing, vigils, boycotts, work and hunger strikes, and more.

One of his most successful campaigns was the Salt March. Britain placed a heavy tax on salt, and it hit India's poor people the hardest. On March 12, 1930, Gandhi marched 240 miles to a town by the sea called Dandi. Thousands of Indians joined the 24-day march. Gandhi broke the law and made his own salt from seawater. His action inspired similar protests across India. Gandhi and about 60,000 Indians were jailed for breaking the Salt Acts. Mahatma Gandhi became a beloved figure around the world.

Gandhi picks up grains of salt by the sea in the town of Dandi.

CHAPTER 2
Civil Rights Activities in the 1950s

The Regional Council of Negro Leadership (RCNL) was based in the Mississippi Delta area. It was started in 1951 by Dr. T.R.M. Howard, a very successful African American surgeon and businessman. The Council's mission was to promote programs of civil rights, self-help, and business ownership. It conducted mass meetings with thousands of people.[1]

Civil rights activist Medgar Evers became its program director. In 1952, Evers organized RCNL's first protest—a boycott in the Delta against gas stations that refused to let nonwhites use their restrooms. Protesters issued 20,000 bumper stickers for supporters to put on their cars. Their slogan was, "Don't Buy Gas Where You Can't Use the Restroom."

The campaign had some success. There were gas stations that added a third "Colored" toilet next to their "White-only" restrooms.[2]

The Murder of Emmett Till Protest Rally
In 1955, while visiting relatives in Mississippi, 14-year-old Emmett Till from Chicago was beaten to death and dumped

Civil rights activist Medgar Evers was born in 1925 in Mississippi. He worked to overturn segregation at the University of Mississippi and became the first field secretary for the NAACP.

CHAPTER TWO

Protesters at the Emmett Till rally

in a river for allegedly whistling at a white woman. Two white men were arrested for the murder. An all-white jury acquitted them. Later, the men bragged about murdering Till in a magazine interview.[3]

Emmett's mother wanted justice. She asked that the casket be open at his funeral. She wanted the world to see his horribly bruised and beaten body. Outrage and sympathy poured in from around the world.[4] The shameful verdict led to boycotts and demonstrations.

On October 11, 1955, a massive rally was held in New York City. Led by the NAACP and the Retail, Wholesale and the Department Store Workers Union, protesters questioned the slaying of Emmett Till. A. Philip Randolph, organizer of the first African American labor union—the Brotherhood of Sleeping Car Porters—gave a powerful speech. He said people needed to fight against racism and social injustice.

Many people view Till's murder as the event that sparked the civil rights movement. The tragedy encouraged more people to join the struggle.

The Montgomery Bus Boycott

Two months later, on December 1, 1955, Rosa Parks, a seamstress in Montgomery, Alabama, rode a city bus. The driver ordered her to give up her seat to a white man. The soft-spoken but fearless woman refused. She was immediately arrested. She had violated the city's racial segregation law: blacks sitting in the back of public buses must give up their seats to white riders if the other front seats were full.

Parks was also the secretary of the local NAACP chapter. Word of her arrest rapidly spread. The city's black leaders quickly organized a one-day boycott of the city's buses. They knew that 70 percent of the bus riders in the city were black. On December 5, 90 percent of the black community did not ride the buses.[5] The boycott was a great success. It led to the formation of the Montgomery Improvement Association (MIA). Its purpose was to mobilize more protests.

Rosa Parks being fingerprinted by police

The MIA appointed as their leader a 26-year-old preacher with a powerful voice named Martin Luther King Jr. He stood at the pulpit of the Holt Street Baptist Church. Thousands of people crowded inside and outside the building. King talked about the bravery of Rosa Parks and the upcoming boycott: "We are not here advocating violence. . . . The only weapon that we have in our hands this evening is the weapon of protest. . . . And we are determined here in Montgomery—to work and fight until justice runs down like water and righteousness like a mighty stream!"[6]

People clapped, stomped their feet, and roared their approval.

King finished his speech with this: "Let us go out with a grim and bold determination that we are going to stick together. . . . When the history books are written . . . somebody will have to say, there lived a race of people, black people . . . who had the moral courage to stand up for their rights."[7]

King was vital in leading the long Montgomery bus boycott. Many other activists joined him, including Bayard Rustin, Jo Ann Robinson, E.D. Nixon, and the Reverend Ralph David Abernathy. King and Abernathy were close

CHAPTER TWO

Martin Luther King on the first bus after the boycott's success

associates. Like James Farmer, they had also studied Mahatma Gandhi's principles of nonviolence.

The bus boycott continued for over twelve months. Montgomery's black citizens were cooperative and supportive of each other. Their solidarity was amazing to behold. Churches organized private taxis and carpools to transport people to work. Thousands of blacks walked miles to work and back home, refusing to ride segregated buses. They sang:

Ain't gonna let nobody
Turn me roun', turn me roun',
Turn me roun',
Gon' keep on walkin',
Keep on a talkin'
Walkin' to the Promised Land.[8]

White resistance was fierce. King's and Nixon's homes were bombed. Carpool drivers were stopped and issued tickets for minor reasons. There were acts of violence, police harassment, and arrests. But the boycotts continued until the MIA was victorious. The U.S. Supreme Court ruled on November 13 that Alabama's bus segregation seating policy was unconstitutional.

On the morning of December 21, 1956, the first integrated bus rolled through Montgomery. As King got on and sat near the front, the bus driver politely greeted him, saying, "We are glad to have you this morning."[9]

The success achieved by MIA inspired bus boycotts across the country. It also thrust Martin Luther King Jr. into the national spotlight.

MUSIC AND THE MOVEMENT

Music played a powerful role in the civil rights movement. There were all types of music, including black spirituals, gospel, folk, rhythm and blues, and jazz. People sang in churches, community meetings, marches, and even in jail. Martin Luther King Jr. called music "the soul of the movement." He said freedom songs "give people new courage and a sense of unity. I think they keep alive faith, a radiant hope in the future, particularly in our most trying hours."[10]

Men, women, and children performed these freedom songs. It was common during protests to hear songs like "Eyes on the Prize," "We Shall Overcome," "Tree of Life," "Oh Freedom," "We Shall Not Be Moved," "This Little Light of Mine," and "Lift Every Voice and Sing."

While many songs were uplifting, some of them captured the tragic events of the era. Billie Holiday's "Strange Fruit" was about the horror of lynching. Jazz musician John Coltrane wrote the emotional instrumental "Alabama" after four black girls were killed in a church bombing in Birmingham. "People Get Ready" by Curtis Mayfield & The Impressions is filled with the promise and excitement of the civil rights movement. "A Change Gonna Come" by Sam Cooke dealt with the struggle and hope for world change.[11]

Sam Cooke

CHAPTER 3
Sit-Ins and Freedom Rides

On February 1, 1960 in Greensboro, North Carolina, four black friends sat down at the segregated Woolworth's white lunch counter and ordered coffee and doughnuts. The men—Ezell Blair, Jr., Franklin McCain, Joseph McNeil, and David Richmond—were freshmen from the all-black North Carolina Agricultural and Technical College. The waitress told them, "I'm sorry, we don't serve you here." A police officer arrived on the scene and paced back and forth behind the freshmen. He slapped his billy club in his hand, not sure what to do. The store manager tried to convince the students to leave, but they politely refused. The peaceful young men sat unserved until the store closed. They told the staff they would be back.[1]

By the time the men returned to campus, everyone knew about their sit-in. Student leaders met with them and organized a follow-up protest. The next day, thirty more black students joined them at the lunch counter. The day after that, so many students, black and white, became a part of the sit-in it disrupted downtown business activities. By the end of the week, the mayor of Greensboro showed up to negotiate the

(From left) Joseph McNeil and Franklin McCain were two of the Greensboro Four. When they came back on February 2, Billy Smith (third from left) and Clarence Henderson (far right), along with about 25 others, joined them.

CHAPTER THREE

student's demands. Media coverage of the event triggered more nonviolent sit-ins throughout the South.

Within two weeks, sit-ins were being held in North Carolina and Virginia. Thirty-one communities in seven states launched this method by the end of the month. But the rapid growth of sit-ins soon led to violent reactions. The white community saw the protesters as "agitators."

People who wanted to participate in sit-ins received training on how to act in a nonviolent manner. Civil rights activist Reverend James Lawson held workshops in Nashville. As the sit-ins spread, angry whites attacked people, yanking them from their stools and punching and kicking them. They dumped catsup, drinks, and food on them. The police harassed protesters, beating them with clubs and throwing them in jail for disorderly conduct. The protesters kept their cool and did not retaliate.

By July, the Greensboro Woolworth's finally served lunch to the original four protesters at the same counter where it all started. The success of the sit-ins and its young protesters grew to be the main focus of the movement. Sit-ins were used to integrate parks, swimming pools, theaters, libraries, and other public facilities.

The Freedom Riders

In 1961, James Farmer, head of the Congress of Racial Equality (CORE), organized a second Journey of Reconciliation. This time it was called the "Freedom Rides." Thirteen trained black and white volunteers left Washington, D.C., on the first Freedom Ride into the South. John Lewis of the Student Non-violent Coordinating Committee (SNCC) and James Peck, a veteran of the 1947 Journey, joined them. Two groups set out on the second journey by bus. The plan was to target facilities on the road, including waiting rooms, restrooms, and restaurants.[2]

The Freedom Riders were attacked outside of Anniston, Alabama. One bus arriving at a depot had its tires slashed and windows smashed. On Mother's Day, May 14, 1961, a mob of Klansman, some still dressed in church

Sit-Ins and Freedom Rides

clothes, firebombed the bus. The riders were trapped inside. A police officer fired his gun into the air and the mob retreated. The bus doors flew open, and Freedom Riders stumbled out and fell to the ground, coughing and gasping for air. Many were taken to the hospital for treatment.

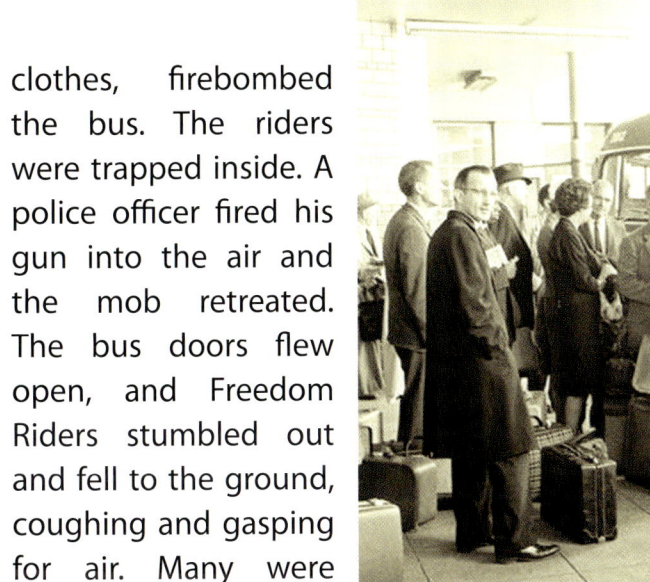

James Farmer (holding briefcase) boards a Freedom Ride bus headed for the Deep South.

James Farmer had a Freedom Ride emblem designed. It was a photo of the burning bus rising out of the flame on the torch of the Statue of Liberty. It became a symbol of the Freedom Ride.

Once the Freedom Riders reached Birmingham, another enraged white mob attacked the riders. Led by the Commissioner of Public Safety, racist Eugene "Bull" Connor, the mob let loose with fists, pipes, chains, and baseball bats. Several riders were severely injured. Hundreds of protesters were jailed and tortured with electric shocks from cattle prods. They were not given any food. Alabama Governor John Patterson argued on television that he could not protect the riders. He called them "a bunch of rabble-rousers."[3]

The Freedom Riders were escorted out of the city, protected by the Justice Department. But the protests did not end there. Their commitment deepened. In Nashville, civil rights activist Diane Nash met with Fred Shuttlesworth, a Birmingham minister and co-founder of the Southern Christian Leadership Conference (SCLC). She told him that her students wanted to come to Birmingham and continue the Freedom Ride.

CHAPTER THREE

Diane Nash and students sing a protest song at the Nashville police station.

Shuttlesworth remarked, "Do you know that the Freedom Riders were almost killed here?"

Nash replied: "Yes, that's exactly why the ride must not be stopped. If they stop us with violence, the movement is dead. We're coming!"[4]

The Nashville students boarded a bus to Birmingham on May 17. They were attacked and harassed by an even larger mob than before. But they kept coming back. The Nashville riders also traveled to Montgomery, Alabama. Finally, Attorney General Robert F. Kennedy ordered in 600 federal marshals to guard the Freedom Riders. The Freedom Riders continued their quest into the state of Mississippi.

That summer, over 300 Freedom Riders were arrested. While trying to work out a deal with the Mississippi Senator, President John F. Kennedy and Attorney General Robert Kennedy asked the civil rights leaders for a "cooling-off" period. Farmer responded: "Blacks have been cooling off for 350 years. If we cool off any more we will be in a deep freeze."[5]

The Freedom Riders achieved their goal. In September 1961, the U.S. Interstate Commerce Commission banned segregated facilities in bus and train stations nationwide.

The South had largely ignored the 1946 ruling that segregation in interstate travel was unconstitutional. Despite the courage of the black and white bus riders during the Journey of Reconciliation, the south maintained its Jim Crow laws. Bus travel remained segregated. Both the Montgomery Bus Boycott and the Freedom Riders were more successful. They had the strength and power of massive protests behind them.

The Reverend James Lawson and His Nonviolent Workshops

Religious student James Lawson was thirty years old when he was jailed for opposing the Korean War. He got out on parole and was sent by his church to India as a missionary. In India he learned about Mahatma Gandhi and how he used passive resistance to battle racial prejudice. When he returned to the United States, Lawson taught Martin Luther King Jr. about Gandhi's nonviolent tactics during the Montgomery Bus Boycott. Lawson began conducting workshops in nonviolence throughout the South.[6] He was teaching in Nashville when four black men launched the sit-in at the Woolworth's lunch counter in Greensboro, North Carolina.

With all the media attention, before the end of the week, over 500 students came to Lawson's workshop. They wanted to be trained to be in the sit-in movement in Nashville. The Nashville sit-in movement soon became known as the largest and most organized of them all. In those very tough workshops, black and white students practiced nonviolent tactics. They learned how to behave when people called them terrible names, hit and knocked them down, blew cigarette smoke into their face, and spit on them. The students had to respond with love and dignity. They were taught: "Don't strike back or curse if abused . . . show yourself courteous and friendly at all times. . . . Remember love and nonviolence."[7] Some of the most famous civil rights leaders were trained in these workshops.

James Lawson (left) with Martin Luther King Jr.

CHAPTER 4
Mass Protests and Marches

In 1963, there were more demonstrations than in any other year. More than 930 demonstrations were held in at least 1,500 southern cities. Scores of additional demonstrations were held in northern and western cities.[1] One of the best-known protests occurred in Birmingham, Alabama's largest city. It was also the most segregated city in America, with a frightening history of racial violence.

Martin Luther King Jr. and SCLC leader Fred Shuttlesworth planned a citywide protest. They wanted to wage war on Jim Crow laws and push for fair hiring. They also wanted to desegregate public places, including schools, lunch counters, bus terminals, elevators, and parks. Shuttlesworth remarked, "We wanted confrontation, nonviolent confrontation to see if it would work on a massive scale. Not for just Birmingham—for the nation."[2]

In early April 1963, thousands of protesters joined the campaign in Birmingham.[3] The city's hostile police commissioner, Eugene "Bull" Connor, again fiercely refused to obey the federal court orders. He did everything in his power

A protester in Birmingham stands with courage against the attack of a police dog. This moment would later be immortalized with a statue in Kelly Ingram Park.

CHAPTER FOUR

to maintain segregation in Birmingham. He closed city parks, swimming pools, playgrounds, and golf courses instead of agreeing to desegregate. The protesters knew the march in Birmingham could be very dangerous. The city had earned the name "Bombingham" because African American houses, churches, and businesses were targeted so often.[4]

King was arrested and thrown into solitary confinement. While there, he wrote "Letter from a Birmingham Jail," a powerful appeal for nonviolent civil disobedience.

The campaign continued, but many adults did not march. They were afraid of being arrested or losing their jobs. The young people carried the baton instead.

On Thursday, May 2, thousands of schoolchildren marched into the city's segregated Kelly Ingram Park. These young troopers were immediately taken to jail. But another "Children's Crusade" showed up and marched the next day. With the jails jam-packed with protesters, Bull Connor took another approach. He ordered the protesters to be sprayed with fire hoses. During

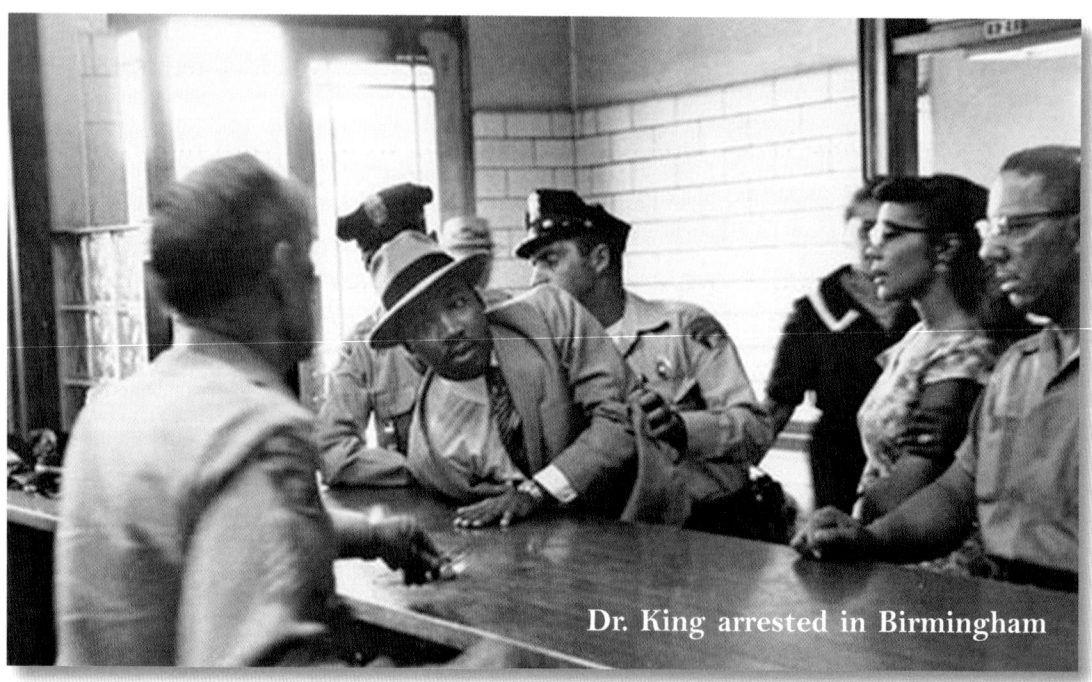

Dr. King arrested in Birmingham

Mass Protests and Marches

Birmingham Commissioner of Public Safety Bull Connor ordered the use of fire hoses on protesters. In 1962, the city of Birmingham voted to replace the position of Commissioner of Public Safety. By June 1963, Bull Connor was out of a job.

their peaceful walk, black high school students were hit with high-pressure jets of water. They were beaten with clubs and attacked by police dogs. Many had to go to the hospital.[5]

The violent images were shown on TV. They exposed millions of Americans to the prejudice African Americans faced daily. Many of these viewers were witnessing this type of racism for the first time. They became sympathetic to the young people who were willing to go to jail for their beliefs.

The Kennedy administration finally made a stronger effort to reduce the crisis. Government officials pressured business leaders in the city to change their policies. As a peaceful resolution, the business leaders agreed to desegregate stores and hire more black workers.

CHAPTER FOUR

Asa Philip Randolph championed labor rights for African Americans. He was the head of the 1963 March on Washington.

The March on Washington

During World War II, defense industries in the United States were growing quickly. Thousands of jobs were available in the defense industry. However, black men and women were not being hired for these jobs. Civil rights leaders agreed to plan a massive march in Washington, D.C. The president of the Brotherhood of Sleeping Car Porters, A. Philip Randolph, thought of the plan for the "March on Washington" movement. Randolph organized the march to pressure President Franklin D. Roosevelt to change these unfair labor practices.

The pressure worked. In 1941, the President issued an executive order banning discrimination in the defense industries. Randolph canceled the march.

Randolph's idea was still strong, and he lived to see his dream turn into reality. Civil rights activist Bayard Rustin organized a tremendous event on the Mall in Washington, D.C. On August 28, 1963, over 200,000 people attended the March on Washington for Jobs and Freedom. In the sweltering afternoon heat, the audience was treated to speeches and music. The grand finale was reserved for Martin Luther King Jr. This was when he delivered his powerful "I Have a Dream" speech. It excited not just the crowd, but the entire country. King was a force that day. His words were both passionate and poetic. After this moving speech, King was hailed as the spokesman for black America.

Mass Protests and Marches

Future congressman and civil rights activist John Lewis (foreground). On March 7, 1965, Lewis led 600 peaceful marchers over the Edmund Pettus Bridge in Selma, Alabama.

The Selma to Montgomery March

In January 1965, the SCLC focused on registering black voters in Selma, Alabama. Governor George Wallace and Sheriff Jim Clark were openly against allowing blacks to vote. Clark proudly wore a badge that stated, "NEVER!" As a result, only 2 percent of Selma's eligible black voters had been registered.

The SCLC announced a massive protest march. It would cover 54 miles, from Selma to Montgomery, the state capital. On Sunday, March 7, six hundred marchers crossed the Edmund Pettus Bridge outside of Selma. Armed troopers attacked them. The troopers, on foot and riding horses, used whips, nightsticks, and tear gas. Dozens of people were injured, including John Lewis, whose skull was fractured. The brutal scene was called "Bloody Sunday."[6]

CHAPTER FOUR

President Lyndon B. Johnson signs the Voting Rights Act into law, guaranteeing African Americans the right to vote. King and other civil rights leaders stand behind him.

The U.S. District Court stepped in and ordered Alabama to permit the march. On March 21, King led over 2,000 people on the three-day journey. This time, they were protected by the U.S. Army and the Alabama National Guard.

President Lyndon B. Johnson signed the Voting Rights Act into law on August 6, 1965. States were no longer allowed to prevent black people from registering to vote.

Johnson also signed the Fair Housing Act of 1968. This act prohibited discrimination in the sale, rental, and financing of homes. The President signed it on April 11, one week after Martin Luther King Jr. had been assassinated in Memphis.

The Bay Area March Against Job Discrimination

In 1960, African American organizations in Berkeley, San Francisco, and Oakland, California, met to form a new group. They created the Ad Hoc Committee To End Racial Discrimination. One of its goals was to end racism in job hiring. Their plan was to pressure businesses to hire more minority employees. White business owners claimed that black workers would scare away their white customers.[7]

In 1963, the Committee organized nonviolent marches and sit-ins throughout the Bay Area. Hundreds of these protesters were arrested.[8] The Committee picketed Mel's Drive-In Diners, San Francisco's Sheraton-Palace Hotel, automobile dealerships, Lucky's grocery stores, and other businesses. They also picketed the Oakland Tribune newspaper building. Although a few people were hired, overall, the Committee's demands were not met. Businesses failed to hire more black workers. In 1967, unemployment was still very high among blacks, especially those under age 25.[9]

In 1963, student members of the Ad Hoc Committee to End Racial Discrimination picketed Mel's Diner.

CHAPTER 5
Modern Civil Rights Protests

This is a Movement, Not a Moment!
— Chant heard at Black Lives Matter protest march in Washington, D.C. (2016)

Even after the civil rights laws were passed in the 1960s, discrimination continued. Meanwhile, Martin Luther King Jr.'s vision of a society where all people have equal rights thrived. It greatly influenced the ongoing civil rights movement. And it prompted people in the United States to protest discrimination in other countries as well as at home.

The Tupelo March and Boycott

In 1976, in the small city of Tupelo, Mississippi, two white police officers severely beat a black man. The man, Eugene Pasto, filed a lawsuit against them, and a federal court ruled in his favor. Outraged by the brutality, black citizens wanted the officers to be fired. White council members disagreed. Instead, they offered to transfer the officers to another department. The black community saw this move as an insult. Several years

In 1978, poultry factory workers went on strike and marched with the United League. They wanted the struggling workers in Tupelo, Mississippi, to be able to form a labor union. They also wanted to end police brutality.

CHAPTER FIVE

Skip Robinson

before, Alfred "Skip" Robinson had formed a grassroots movement named the United League. Its goal was to champion the rights of poor African Americans in Mississippi.[1] The United League stepped in to help the people of Tupelo.

On March 11, 1978, more than 400 people demonstrated against the police brutality. Robinson called for a second march in June. The black community would also boycott white-owned businesses in downtown Tupelo. The demonstrators demanded that more black people be hired across the city.

The Ku Klux Klan (KKK) planned a countermarch on the same day. The National Guard stationed 65 riot-clad police along the planned march route. However, conflict was avoided. The 600 United League marchers started at 12:30 p.m., and the KKK's march of around 200 people did not start until 2:30 p.m. The United League boycotts remained until the city employed more black workers.[2]

The Free South Africa Movement

On Thanksgiving eve in 1984, four well-known black activists walked into the South African Embassy on Massachusetts Avenue in Washington, D.C. They conducted a sit-in there. They demanded an end to apartheid, a brutal system of racial injustice in South Africa. The country had 23 million black citizens and 4.5 million whites. The government, run by whites, oppressed the black citizens in many ways. The races had limited contact. All places, including whole neighborhoods, were separated according to race. Mixed-race families were torn apart. Black farmers were forced off their land, landing them in poverty. And black people were not allowed to vote. Nelson Mandela led a freedom movement there, but he was arrested. By 1984, he had been a political prisoner for 20 years.[3]

Modern Civil Rights Protests

Three of the embassy protesters were handcuffed to police cars and then jailed. They were Randall Robinson, founder and director of the policy group TransAfrica; Mary Frances Berry, U.S. Civil Rights Commissioner; and D.C. Congressman Walter E. Fauntroy. Eleanor Holmes Norton, Georgetown University Law Professor, had left before the arrests. She told the press what happened.

The embassy arrests became international news, and the Free South Africa Movement (FSAM) was born in the United States. Daily protests began outside the embassy and in South African consulates around the county. Within the next couple of years, six thousand demonstrators were arrested.

There was a huge number of grassroots actions in the churches, on campuses, and among the unions. Coretta Scott King and Rosa Parks joined the demonstrations as the crowds sang, "We Shall Overcome."[4] The intense

Coretta Scott King joined the protests against apartheid in South Africa. She and others were arrested for demonstrating within 500 feet of the South African Embassy.

35

CHAPTER FIVE

public pressure forced President Ronald Reagan to publicly condemn apartheid.

During this period, protesters, who were called "messengers," chanted, "Free Nelson Mandela!" Drums and dancers demonstrated on embassy grounds. Celebrities such as tennis star Arthur Ashe and musician Stevie Wonder flew in to join the protests. They were also arrested. College students pressured their boards of trustees to sell the stock they owned in companies doing business with the South African government.

In 1986, the U.S. Congress passed the Comprehensive Anti-Apartheid Act, and sanctions were placed on South Africa. In 1990, more than 160 U.S. companies stopped doing business with South Africa. It cost South Africa billions of dollars. Finally, Nelson Mandela was released from prison. In 1994, South Africa adopted a new constitution. It gave blacks the right to vote and called for the election of a president. They voted for Nelson Mandela.[5]

In 1993, Nelson Mandela (right) and South African President F.W. de Klerk were given the Nobel Peace Prize. A year later, Mr. Mandela replaced him as president.

Modern Civil Rights Protests

The Afton "Lie-Down" Protest

In 1982, ten yellow dump trucks drove to a new landfill site at Afton, in rural Warren County, North Carolina. The trucks carried six tons of contaminated soil with cancer-inducing toxins. At the site stood sixty riot-equipped patrol officers ready to confront over a hundred black protesters. The marchers lay down on the road in front of the approaching trucks. The trucks stopped, but the officers arrested 55 demonstrators to clear the road. The trucks then dropped their toxic loads.

Children grab signs to join in the Afton protest to stop dump trucks from hauling toxic soil into the area in 1982.

The Afton "lie-down" developed into a national movement. The next morning, more protesters arrived and lay down on the road. Local activists and civil rights leaders around the country flew in. Over five hundred demonstrators were arrested, and the lie-down protests made the national news.

The local pastor, Luther Brown said: "We know why they picked us. . . . Because it's a poor county and mostly black. . . . Nobody thought people like us would make a fuss."[6]

The protesters could not stop the landfills. Trucks dumped over forty thousand cubic yards of toxic soil. Still, the story received a huge amount of publicity.

Because of Afton, in 1991, black activists widened their focus to include environmental racism. Hundreds of activists met for the First National

CHAPTER FIVE

People of Color Environmental Leadership Summit. Demonstrations put pressure on the federal government. Veteran civil rights activist John Lewis and Senator Al Gore introduced an environmental bill to Congress. When Gore became vice president, President Bill Clinton signed an executive order. The order directed federal agencies to identify and address any bad environmental effects their programs would have on people of color.[7]

The Million Man March

On October 16, 1995, an estimated 850,000 African American men attended the "Million Man March." The March was held at the Mall in Washington, D.C. It called for black men to unify and address the ills of the black community. The goal was for black men to take responsibility for their lives, their families, and their communities, and to build a base of black political power. Besides marching, more than 10,000 black men registered to vote that day.[8]

Many religious groups, businesses, schools, and community organizations participated in the march. Speakers and entertainers included event organizer Louis Farrakhan, the Reverend Jesse Jackson, Rosa Parks, Dick Gregory, Stevie Wonder, and Maya Angelou.

Elaine Steele, Rosa Parks, Ayindé Jean-Baptiste and others join the Million Man March in Washington, D.C.

The Million Woman March

In 1997, the Million Woman March took place on October 25. It is estimated that 750,000 African American women from across the country

gathered to march on the Ben Franklin Parkway in Philadelphia. The march started at the Liberty Bell and ended on the steps of the Philadelphia Museum of Art. Grassroots activists Phile Chionesu and Asia Coney organized the march. Its mission was to bring women together to discuss such issues as strengthening black families, finding a common voice in politics and civil rights, and battling the negative images of black women in popular culture and the media.[9]

The goal of the Million Woman March in 1997 was to rebuild black communities. An estimated 750,000 women gathered to march on the Ben Franklin Parkway in Philadelphia.

Black Lives Matter Protests

During the summer of 2013, three community organizers—Alicia Garza, Patrisse Cullors, and Opal Tometi—founded the Black Lives Matter (BLM) movement. They shared a passion for fighting social injustice, and they found each other on social media after the murder of Trayvon Martin. Martin was an unarmed seventeen-year-old who was killed by George Zimmerman, a neighborhood watch coordinator. Zimmerman was later acquitted of the killing. The verdict produced tremendous outrage in the black community.

The women understood the history of the nonviolent struggle of the civil rights movement, and they recognized the power of social media to mobilize the community. On August 9, 2014, eighteen-year-old Michael Brown was killed by police officer Darren Wilson. This time, BLM was ready.

CHAPTER FIVE

In 2016, Black Lives Matter shut down city streets in downtown Baltimore with peaceful rallies, marches, and sit-ins.

More than 500 BLM members from cities throughout the nation gathered to protest and demonstrate against the police shooting. Protesters chanted, "Hands up! Don't shoot!" News stories about these events pushed the issue of police brutality onto the national and international stage.[10]

Between 2014 and 2015, Black Lives Matter chapters had organized more than 950 protest demonstrations against police actions involving the deaths of black citizens.[11] Their demonstrations have prompted investigations into police misconduct across the country. In 2014, the U.S. Congress enacted the Death and Custody Reporting Act. The Act requires states to document and report all deaths at the hands of police that occur during an arrest.

Black Lives Matter protests have continued around the country. In 2016, Alton Sterling was shot by police in Baton Rouge, Louisiana. Hundreds of people gathered to protest, and one hundred were arrested. Among them was Ieshia Evans, a nurse and mother, who stood stock still while police in riot gear handcuffed her. She later wrote, "I wasn't afraid. I took a stand in Baton Rouge because enough is enough."[12]

Ieshia Evans stands calmly as riot police advance during a Black Lives Matter protest.

More Heroines of Civil Rights

Dorothy Height
President Barack Obama called Dorothy Height "the godmother of the Civil Rights Movement."[13] In 1946 Height helped to direct the integration of all the YWCA Centers. She was President of the National Council for Negro Women for 40 years. She formed the Center for Racial Justice in 1965. She helped to organize the March on Washington. She also organized workshops to help freedom schools and provided help to poor families.

Fannie Lou Hamer
Fannie Lou Hamer came from a large family of Mississippi sharecroppers. In 1962 she became a civil rights activist. She championed registering black people to vote in Mississippi. For her courageous efforts she was threatened, shot at, arrested, and beaten so badly she suffered from kidney damage for the rest of her life. She helped establish the Mississippi Freedom Democratic Party. Besides her devotion to helping families in need, she is remembered for her dynamic and fiery speech at the Democratic National Convention in 1964. She spoke about the resistance and violence she and other blacks experienced in Mississippi while they were trying to register voters. By the time she finished, she had become the heart of the convention.

TIMELINE

1863 President Abraham Lincoln signs the Emancipation Proclamation, which frees the slaves in the United States.

1868 The Fourteenth Amendment is passed: African Americans may not be denied equal protection or due process of law.

1870 The Fifteenth Amendment is passed, giving black men the right to vote.

1875 Civil Rights Act of 1875 prohibits racial discrimination and guarantees equal access to public accommodations.

1877 Reconstruction ends in the South. Civil rights for blacks are no longer protected.

1896 *Plessey v. Ferguson* holds that racial segregation is constitutional. It opens the door for Jim Crow laws in the South.

1909 The National Association for the Advancement of Colored People is founded. Its publication *The Crisis* is launched.

1914 Marcus Garvey establishes the Universal Negro Improvement Association "to promote the spirit of race pride."

1941 President Theodore Roosevelt signs an executive order that bans discrimination against minorities in defense contracts.

1948 President Harry S. Truman issues an executive order integrating the U.S. Armed forces.

1954 In *Brown v. Board of Education of Topeka Kansas*, the U.S. Supreme Court rules that racial segregation in schools is unconstitutional.

1955 Emmett Till is murdered. Rosa Parks refuses to give up her seat at the front of the "colored section" of a bus in Montgomery, Alabama, to a white passenger, defying a southern custom. It leads to a successful year-long bus boycott led by Martin Luther King Jr.

1957 The Southern Christian Leaders Conference is established. Federal troops are sent to protect nine African-American students from white mobs trying to block integration at Central High School in Little Rock, Arkansas.

1960 Four black students in Greensboro, North Carolina, begin a sit-in at a segregated Woolworth's lunch counter. The event triggers nonviolent protests throughout the South. The Student Nonviolent Coordinating Committee is founded, providing young blacks a place in the civil rights movement.

1961 Congress of Racial Equality (CORE) organizes the Freedom Rides into the South to test new laws prohibiting segregation in interstate travel facilities. Bus riders are attacked by angry mobs.

1963 Martin Luther King writes "Letter from Birmingham Jail." At the March on Washington for Jobs and Freedom, King delivers his famous "I Have a Dream" speech. Four black girls are killed when a bomb explodes at a church in Birmingham. Mississippi Freedom Summer voter education and registration project begins—two white and one black student volunteers are murdered. President John F. Kennedy is assassinated.

TIMELINE

1964 President Lyndon B. Johnson signs the Civil Rights Act. Martin Luther King Jr. receives the Nobel Peace Prize.

1965 The Voting Rights Act is signed into law. Black nationalist Malcolm X is assassinated. The Watts section of Los Angeles explodes into six days of rioting. On Bloody Sunday, troops attack the Selma to Montgomery marchers. Another larger march is successful.

1966 The Black Panthers are founded by Huey Newton and Bobby Seale. Stokely Carmichael, head of the SNCC, coins the term "Black Power" during a voter registration drive in Mississippi.

1967 President Johnson appoints African American Thurgood Marshall to the Supreme Court. The Supreme Court rules in *Loving v. Virginia* that prohibiting interracial marriage is unconstitutional.

1968 Martin Luther King Jr. is assassinated in Memphis. The Civil Rights Act of 1968 is signed by President Johnson. Shirley Chisholm becomes the first black female U.S. Representative.

1971 The Supreme Court in *Swann v. Charlotte-Mecklenburg Board of Education* upholds busing as a legitimate means for achieving integration of public schools.

1988 Congress passes the Civil Rights Restoration Act, overriding President Ronald Reagan's veto. It expands nondiscrimination laws within private institutions that receive federal funds.

1992 Race riots erupt after a Los Angeles jury acquits four white police officers of the beating of Rodney King.

1994 After worldwide protests against apartheid, South Africa adopts a new constitution and elects Nelson Mandela as president.

2001 Colin Powell becomes the first African American U.S. Secretary of State.

2005 Condolezza Rice becomes the first black female U.S. Secretary of State.

2008 Barack Obama is the first African American elected president of the United States.

2013 After the man who killed Trayvon Martin is acquitted, Alicia Garza, Patrisse Cullors, and Opal Tometi form Black Lives Matter.

2014 The killing of unarmed 18-year-old Michael Brown by officer Darren Wilson sparks protests in Ferguson, Missouri, and cities across the United States. Congress enacts the Death and Custody Reporting Act.

2017 In January nearly 2,000 mostly black protesters march near Washington's Martin Luther King Jr. Memorial for minority rights and to preserve the Affordable Care Act (Obamacare), which President Donald J. Trump has threatened to eliminate.

CHAPTER NOTES

Chapter 1: Civil Rights Protests—The Beginnings

1. "Confrontational Abolitionism," *The Abolition Seminar.* http://www.abolitionseminar.org/confrontational-abolitionism/
2. "Oldest and Boldest," http://www.naacp.org/oldest-and-boldest/
3. Patricia Sullivan. *Lift Every Voice: The NAACP and the Making of the Civil Rights Movement* (New York: The New Press, 2009), pp. 48–49.
4. Dick Lehr, "When 'Birth of a Nation' Sparked a Riot in Boston," *Boston Globe*, October 5, 2016, https://www.bostonglobe.com/ideas/2016/10/05/when-birth-nation-sparked-riot-boston/bN9S0ltko6QyRlQiJcr9KJ/story.html
5. Sullivan, pp. 68–69.
6. "The First Massive African American Protest in U.S. History Was Led by Children Marching Against Lynching in the Silent Protest Parade," *Black Then*, November 11, 2016, https://blackthen.com/first-massive-african-american-protest-in-u-s-history-was-led-by-children-marching-against-lynching-in-the-silent-protest-parade/
7. James Farmer, *Lay Bare the Heart: An Autobiography of the Civil Rights Movement* (Fort Worth: Texas Christian University Press, 1985), pp. 106–107.
8. George Hauser, "The Freedom Rides: From Project to Mass Movement." Fellowship of Reconciliation USA Archives. http://archives.forusa.org/blogs/george-houser/freedom-rides-project-mass-movement/8744
9. CORE: "George Houser (1927–) Co-Founder, Congress of Racial Equality," http://www.congressofracialequality.org/george-houser.html
10. "Mahatma Gandhi," Biography, http://www.biography.com/people/mahatma-gandhi-9305898
11. Ibid.
12. "Non-violence," BBC Ethics Guide, 2014, http://www.bbc.co.uk/ethics/war/against/nonviolence.shtml

Chapter 2: Civil Rights Activities in the 1950s

1. "May 1952: RCNL Holds First Mass Meeting in Mississippi Delta." Digital SNCC Gateway. https://snccdigital.org/events/rcnl-holds-first-mass-meeting-mississippi-delta/
2. "Regional Council of Negro Leadership Established in Mississippi." Veterans of the Civil Rights Movement—History and Timeline, 1951–1953. http://www.crmvet.org/tim/timhis51.htm
3. Steven Kasher, *The Civil Rights Movement: A Photographic History, 1954–68* (New York: Abbeville Press Publishers, 2000), p. 11.
4. Yvonne Ryan, *Roy Wilkins: The Quiet Revolutionary and the NAACP* (Lexington: The University Press of Kentucky, 2014), p. 55.
5. Ryan, pp. 55–56.
6. Taylor Branch, *The King Years: Historic Moments in the Civil Rights Movement* (New York, Simon & Schuster, 2013), pp. 8–11.
7. Kasher, p. 35.
8. James Farmer, *Lay Bare the Heart: An Autobiography of the Civil Rights Movement* (Fort Worth: Texas Christian University Press, 1985), p. 185.
9. Martin Luther King, Jr. *The Autobiography of Martin Luther King, Jr.* Edited by Clayborne Carson (New York: Hachette Book Group, 1998), n.p.
10. "Hope for America: Performers, Politics and Pop Culture Political Songs," Library of Congress, https://www.loc.gov/exhibits/hope-for-america/political-songs.html
11. "Top 10 Civil Rights Protest Songs of all Time," NEWSONE, n.d., https://newsone.com/1460645/top-10-civil-rights-protest-songs-of-all-time/

Chapter 3: Sit-Ins and Freedom Rides

1. Steven Kasher, *The Civil Rights Movement: A Photographic History, 1954–68* (New York: Abbeville Press Publishers, 2000), pp. 66-68.
2. James Farmer, *Lay Bare the Heart: An Autobiography of the Civil Rights Movement*

CHAPTER NOTES

(Fort Worth: Texas Christian University Press, 1985), pp. 196–197.
3. Kasher, pp. 75–76.
4. Ibid.
5. Ibid.
6. Kasher, p. 69.
7. "Jim Lawson Conducts Nonviolence Workshops in Nashville," SNCC Digital Gateway, https://snccdigital.org/events/jim-lawson-conducts-nonviolent-workshops-in-nashville/

Chapter 4: Mass Protests and Marches
1. Stephen Tuck, *We Ain't What We Ought to Be: The Black Freedom Struggle From Emancipation to Obama* (Cambridge: Belknap Press, 2010), p. 295.
2. Steven Kasher, *The Civil Rights Movement: A Photographic History, 1954–68* (New York: Abbeville Press Publishers, 2000), p. 88.
3. Yvonne Ryan, *Roy Wilkins: The Quiet Revolutionary and the NAACP* (Lexington: The University Press of Kentucky, 2014), p. 108.
4. Kasher, p. 88.
5. Tuck, pp. 293–294.
6. Ryan, pp. 146–147.
7. "Civil Rights Marches Against Hiring Practices," Picture This, http://picturethis.museumca.org/timeline/unforgettable-change-1960s/civil-rights/info
8. Carl Nolte, "S.F. Palace Hotel Sit-in Helped Start Revolution 50 years ago," *SFGate*, March 1, 2014, http://www.sfgate.com/bayarea/article/S-F-Palace-Hotel-sit-in-helped-start-revolution-5279160.php
9. "Civil Rights Marches Against Hiring Practices," Picture This, http://picturethis.museumca.org/timeline/unforgettable-change-1960s/civil-rights/info

Chapter 5: Modern Civil Rights Protests
1. Stephen Tuck, *We Ain't What We Ought to Be: The Black Freedom Struggle from Emancipation to Obama* (Cambridge: Belknap Press, 2010), p. 369.

2. "KKK/United League March," Mississippi Civil Rights Project. http://mscivilrightsproject.org/lee/event-lee/kkkunited-league-march/
3. Krissah Thompson, "On Mandela Day, D.C. Founders of Free South Africa Movement Look Back." *The Washington Post*, July 17, 2013. https://www.washingtonpost.com/lifestyle/style/on-mandela-day-dc-founders-of-free-south-africa-movement-look-back/2013/07/17/61db5a5e-eee1-11e2-a1f9-ea873b7e0424_story.html?utm_term=.83d56b7f5f2d
4. Tuck, pp. 379–380.
5. Thompson.
6. Tuck, pp. 383–384.
7. Ibid., p. 385.
8. "Million Man March, 1995," Blackpast.org. http://www.blackpast.org/aah/million-man-march-1995
9. "Million Woman March, 1997." BlackPast.org Blog. http://www.blackpast.org/aah/million-woman-march-1997
10. "Black Lives Matter: The Growth of a New Social Justice Movement." http://www.blackpast.org/perspectives/black-lives-matter-growth-new-social-justice-movement
11. Ibid.
12. Ieshia Evans, "I Wasn't Afraid. I Took a Stand in Baton Rouge Because Enough Is Enough." *The Guardian*, July 22, 2016, https://www.theguardian.com/commentisfree/2016/jul/22/i-wasnt-afraid-i-took-a-stand-in-baton-rouge-because-enough-is-enough
13. Jesse Lee, "The Godmother of the Civil Rights Movement." White House Press Release, April 20, 2010, https://obamawhitehouse.archives.gov/blog/2010/04/20godmother-civil-rights-movement

FURTHER READING

Works Consulted

Branch, Taylor. *The King Years: Historic Moments in the Civil Rights Movement.* New York: Simon & Schuster, 2013.

Farmer, James. *Lay Bare the Heart: An Autobiography of the Civil Rights Movement.* Fort Worth: Texas Christian University Press. 1986.

Friedman, Monroe. *Consumer Boycotts: Effecting Change Through the Marketplace and Media.* New York: Routledge, 1999.

Kasher, Steven. *The Civil Rights Movement: A Photographic History, 1954–68.* New York: Abbeville Press Publishers. 1996.

King, Martin Luther, Jr. *The Autobiography of Martin Luther King, Jr.* Edited by Clayborne Carson. New York: Hachette Book Group, 1998.

Ryan, Yvonne. *Roy Wilkins: The Quiet Revolutionary And The NAACP.* Lexington: University Press of Kentucky. 2014.

Sullivan, Patricia. *Lift Every Voice: The NAACP and the Making of the Civil Rights Movement.* New York: The New Press, 2009.

Tuck, Stephen. *We Ain't What We Ought to Be: The Black Freedom Struggle from Emancipation to Obama.* Cambridge: The Belknap Press, 2010.

Books

Adamson, Heather. *The Civil Rights Movement: An Interactive History Adventure (You Choose: History).* North Mankato, MN: Capstone Press, 2016.

Feldstein, Ruth. *How It Feels to Be Free: Black Women Entertainers and the Civil Rights Movement.* New York: Oxford University Press, 2013.

Lewis, John. *March: Book Three.* Marietta: Top Shelf Productions, 2016.

Shelton, Paula Young. *Child of the Civil Rights Movement.* Decorah, IA: Dragonfly Books. 2013.

Weatherford, Carole Boston. *Voice of Freedom: Fannie Lou Hamer: The Spirit of the Civil Rights Movement.* Somerville, MA: Candlewick Press, 2015.

Internet Reading

African-American Civil Rights Movement. Ducksters—Civil Rights.
   http://www.ducksters.com/history/civil_rights/african-american_civil_rights_movement.php

Civil Rights Movement. John F. Kennedy Presidential Library And Museum.
   https://www.jfklibrary.org/JFK/JFK-in-History/Civil-Rights-Movement.aspx

"The Legacy of the Civil Rights Movement." Virginia Historical Society.
   http://www.vahistorical.org/collections-and-resources/virginia-history-explorer/civil-rights-movement-virginia/legacy-civil

"March On Washington." History for Kids.
   http://www.historyforkids.net/march-on-washington.html

"The Selma Marches for Voting Freedom." Social Studies for Kids.
   http://www.socialstudiesforkids.com/articles/ushistory/selma-montgomerymarches.htm

Zimbler, Suzanne. "Sitting Down to Take a Stand." Time For Kids.
   http://www.timeforkids.com/news/sitting-down-take-stand/5426

GLOSSARY

abolitionist (ab-uh-LIH-shuh-nist)—A person who wants to end slavery.

acquit (uh-KWIT)—To declare that a person is not guilty of a crime.

agitator (AD-jih-tay-ter)—Someone who stirs unrest or controversy.

boycott (BOY-kot)—To refuse to buy, use, or participate in something as a way of protesting.

censor (SEN-ser)—To review books, movies, or other forms of communication in order to remove things that might be objectionable or harmful to society.

disobedience (dis-oh-BEE-dee-unts)—Refusal to obey laws or rules.

grassroots—Starting with the ordinary people in a society or organization.

interstate (IN-ter-stayt)—Involving more than one state.

Jim Crow laws—Laws that discriminated against blacks in the United States; unfair treatment of blacks through segregation.

mobilize (MOH-bul-yz)—To bring people together for an important action.

petition (peh-TIH-shun)—A formal written request made to a person in authority or organization.

reconciliation (reh-kun-sil-ee-AY-shun)—The act of bringing people or groups back together as friends after a disagreement.

resolution (reh-zuh-LOO-shun)—An answer or solution to a conflict or problem.

retaliate (ree-TAL-ee-ayt)—To do something bad to someone who has hurt you; to seek revenge.

sanctions (SANK-shuns)—Formal punishments, such as refusing to trade, used against a government in order to enforce a law.

segregate (SEH-greh-gayt)—To separate people because of their race or religion.

solidarity (sah-luh-DAYR-ih-tee)—A feeling of unity between people who have the same interests and goals.

stereotype (STAYR-ee-oh-typ)—An often unfair and untrue belief that people have about a particular group of people.

PHOTO CREDITS: Pp. 5, 9, 38—Loc.gov; p. 13—FBI.gov; p. 16—innercitylady; p.25—NPS.gov; pp. 33, 34—fortunateson.us; p. 40—John Lucia, ThankHerForSurviving All other photos—Public Domain. Every measure has been taken to find all copyright holders of material used in this book. In the event any mistakes or omissions have happened within, attempts to correct them will be made in future editions of the book.

INDEX

Abernathy, Ralph David   15
Ad Hoc Committee to End Racial Discrimination   31
Afton lie-down protest   37
Berry, Mary Frances   35
Birth of a Nation   4, 6
Black Lives Matter   32, 39, 40
Blair, Ezell Jr.   18
Bloody Sunday   29
Brown, Luther   37
Clark, Jim   29
Clinton, Bill   38
Coltrane, John   17
Committee of Racial Equality (CORE)   8–9
Connor, Eugene "Bull"   21, 24, 26, 27
Cooke, Sam   17
Du Bois, W.E.B.   6, 7
East St. Louis Riots   6, 7
Evers, Medgar   12, 13
Farmer, James   8, 16, 20, 21
Farrakhan, Louis   38
Fauntroy, Walter E.   35
Felmet, Joe   9
First National People of Color Environmental Leadership Summit   37–38
freedom riders   18, 20, 21, 22, 42
Free South Africa Movement (FSAM)   35
Gandhi, Mahatma   8, 10, 11, 16, 23
Gore, Al   38
Greensboro Four   19
Griffith, D.W.   6
Hamer, Fannie Lou   41
Height, Dorothy   41
Holliday, Billie   17
Houser, George   8, 9
Howard, T.R.M.   12
Jackson, Jessie   38
Jack Spratt Diner   8, 9
Johnson, Andrew   9
Johnson, James Weldon   7
Johnson, Lyndon B.   30
Journey of Reconciliation   9, 20, 22
Kelly Ingram Park   25, 26
Kennedy, John F.   22, 27
Kennedy, Robert F.   22
King, Coretta Scott   35
King, Martin Luther, Jr.   10, 15, 16, 17, 23, 24, 28, 30, 32,
Ku Klux Klan   6, 34
Lawson, James   20, 23
Lewis, John   20, 29, 38
Mandela, Nelson   34, 36
March on Washington   28, 41
Mayfield, Curtis   17
McCain, Franklin   18
McNeil, Joseph   18
Million Man March   38
Million Woman March   38–39
Montgomery Bus Boycott   14, 15, 16, 22, 23
Montgomery Improvement Association (MIA)   15–16
Moscowitz, Henry   6
Nash, Diane   21, 22
National Association for the Advancement of Colored People (NAACP)   4, 6, 7, 14, 15
Nixon, E.D.   15, 16
Norton, Eleanor Holmes   35
Ovington, Mary White   6
Rosa Parks   14–15, 35, 38
Pasto, Eugene   32
Patterson, John   21
Peck, James   20
Phillips, Wendell   5
Randolph, A. Philip   14, 28
Reagan, Ronald   36
Richmond, David   18
Robinson, Alfred "Skip"   34
Regional Council of Negro Leadership (RCNL)   12
Robinson, Jo Ann   15
Robinson, Randall   35
Roodenko, Igal   9
Rustin, Bayard   9, 15, 28
Salt March   11
Shuttlesworth, Fred   21, 22, 24
Sims, Thomas   5
Sit-Ins   11, 18, 19, 20, 21, 34
Southern Christian Leadership Conference (SCLC)   21, 24, 29
Student Non-Violent Coordinating Committee (SNCC)   20
Till, Emmett   12, 14
Trotter, William Monroe   6
United League   33, 34
Wallace, George   29
Wells-Barnett, Ida B.   6
Wilson, Woodrow   6